My Sister Emma

Written by Gina Conger

Illustrated by Ash Jackson

This book is dedicated to Daniel, Mom & Pop, Nana, Grandpa, Leslie, Tasha, and the whole family for always inspiring me to follow my dreams.
To my siblings, Bryson, Veronica, R&R, and all the littles reach for the stars; they are closer than you think.

It's a warm summer day, and the sun is shining. "It is a perfect day to go to the park. Grab your jacket, Nathan, let's go!" says my older brother Zach. "Can Emma come too?" I ask. "Of course," he replies.

I rush up the stairs to find my sister Emma
And Mom.
"Mom, can Zach take Em and me to the park?"

Mom grabs Emma's communication board and holds it up to her. "What do you say, Em? Want to go to the park with your brothers?" "T-O-T-A-L-L-Y, totally," Mom says out loud as Emma spells by pointing to each letter on the board. "Awesome! I'll grab your jacket", I say. Emma starts making noises and twisting her fingers really fast. She does that sometimes when she's happy.

I grab our jackets and head toward the door. "Don't forget Emma's backpack and make sure her headphones and communication board are in there!" yells Zach. "Oh, yeah!" I rush back upstairs to grab them!

Emma doesn't always like to wear headphones,
but they help her stay calm when things
get too noisy.

When we get to the park, Zach heads to the Basketball court, and Emma runs towards a tree. She doesn't seem to be interested in the Playground or playing with the other children. I follow her.

Emma grabs a few dry leaves and crumples them up in her hand, making noises as she does it. She loves watching them float out of her hand and away with the wind. When you take the time to look at it, it really does look beautiful. Emma notices a lot of details and beautiful things that I usually don't see until she points them out.

It doesn't take long before some kids run up to Emma. "Hey, what are you doing?" But Emma doesn't say anything. I remember we brought her communication board, "Hold on," I say, "Emma, will you take off your backpack?" She takes it off, hands it to me, and I pull out her communication board.

I stand on Emma's right side and hold the communication board up, just like Mom showed me, saying each letter Emma points to out loud and writing them down in the notebook as we go.

"W-H-A-T-S

U-P

I-T-S

C-A-L-L-E-D

S-T-I-M-M-I-N-G

B-R-O

E-X-P-L-A-I-N," spells Emma.

I read the words out loud, "What's up? It's called stimming bro explain."

"Wow, that was so cool! I can't believe she spelled that! Why doesn't she talk?" asks one kid, "And what is she doing with those leaves?" yells a kid from the back.

"My sister has autism; her body doesn't always listen to her brain, so it can be hard for her to talk with her mouth. She mostly spells on this board to communicate with us. She loves crunching up the leaves and watching them float in the wind. Come check it out! Show them, Em!" I say. They come over and watch her. "Awesome, want to come to play hide-and-seek?" One of them asks.

"What do you say Emma, want to play hide-and-seek?" I ask as I hold the communication board up to her.

"N-O

T-H-A-N-K-S

T-H-O-U-G..."

Suddenly, Emma looks up and starts running into the open field. "No, thanks though," I say. "Sorry, got to go!" I yell back at the kids as I run away.

I finally catch up to her. "What is it Emma? Are you alright?" She doesn't respond, she just looks up at the sky. That's when I hear it, a plane.

I should have known, Emma loves planes, and she always hears them before I do. I wonder what else she hears that I don't.

"Where do you think they are headed Em?" She doesn't answer, but I know she hears me.

MMMMMM The humming of the plane flying overhead is so loud, it drowns out every other noise in the park.
Suddenly, Emma imagines her feet float right off the ground. She flys all the way to the clouds and waves at the pilot.

I hear Zach call. "Time to go, Em, let's put on
your backpack."
I help her put on her backpack, and
We run
to our brother.
"I can't wait to tell Mom and Dad about how we
spelled together today, Emma!"

CPSIA information can be obtained
at www.ICGtesting.com
Printed in the USA
BVHW021704160321
602551BV00033B/660

9 780578 863269